P9-AGR-870

Reycraft Books
55 Fifth Avenue
New York, NY 10003
Reycraftbooks.com

Dedicated to Donna and Angela and all who foster pets.
—A. W.

Reycraft Books is a trade imprint and trademark of Newmark Learning, LLC.
Text copyright © 2022 Annette Whipple
Illustration copyright © 2022 Reycraft Books
Expert review provided by Justin Yesilonis, DVM, CVA.

Educators and Librarians: Our books may be purchased in bulk for promotional, educational, or business use.
Please contact sales@reycraftbooks.com.

Library of Congress Control Number: 2022906692

ISBN: 978-1-4788-7957-2

Photograph credits: Page 6: Nature Picture Library/Alamy; Page 8C: Cordelia Molloy/Science Source; Page 17: Imagebroker/Alamy; Page 21B: sylvia born/Alamy; Page 21D: dpa picture alliance/Alamy; Page 28C: State Archives of Florida/Florida Memory/Alamy; Page 29B: STEVE GSCHMEISSNER/Science Source; All other images from Shutterstock and Getty Images

Illustration credits: Page 3, 5, 7, 9, 11, 13, 15, 17, 19, 21, 23, 25: JuanbJuan Oliver

Production Artist: Loren E. Mack

Printed in Dongguan, China. 8557/0722/19331

10 9 8 7 6 5 4 3 2 1

First Edition Hardcover published by Reycraft Books 2022.

Reycraft Books and Newmark Learning, LLC. support diversity and the First Amendment, and celebrate the right to read.

MEOW!
The Truth About Cats

ANNETTE WHIPPLE

Whose Whiskers Are These?

THE SWISHING TAIL.

THE TWITCHING EARS.

THE RUMBLING PURR.

Cats often sleep all day, ignore our affection, and scratch the furniture. When they act like this, it can be hard to understand these feline pets. But as we get to know cats, we realize they need us as much as we need them.

Kitty Corner

I'm a bit shy but still hope to find my fur-ever family.

Do Cats
Need People?

Tabby Cat

Cats are a bit like people. Some keep to themselves. Others are social. Some are fearful. Others are bold. Each cat is an individual.

A cat's early life influences how it interacts with people later. Ages 2–7 weeks are the most important time for a kitten to be exposed to lots of gentle people and situations. Then it's more likely to grow up to be a social kitty.

Though cats can be self-sufficient, indoor cats rely on people for food, water, and a clean litter box. Cats need space and time to relax, but they also need some entertainment.

Siamese Cat

White Persian

Ginger Cat

Maine Coon

Keep your finger out.

If I touch it with my nose, I'm "feline" friendly. Now you can pet me.

5

British Shorthair

Why Do Mother Cats Carry Kittens By The Neck?

A newborn kitten can't move much on its own. So, when the baby needs to be moved, the mama cat picks it up by the scruff, or back of its neck. When held by the loose skin, the kitten relaxes and goes limp. This makes it easier for the mama to move her kitten.

Kittens rely on their mother for everything. At birth, kittens don't breathe until their mother licks them. The mother feeds them and keeps them warm. By the time the kittens are two weeks old, they open their eyes and begin to hear and explore. Soon they run and wrestle. Playing helps kittens learn to hunt and to get along with other cats.

Kitty Corner

After my kittens go to the bathroom, we don't leave any mess behind. I clean it up with a little lick.

No toilet paper needed!

WHAT GOOD ARE WHISKERS?

Scottish Fold

Whiskers grow above cats' mouths. They have similar hairs on their chin, cheeks, above their eyes, and on their front legs.

Cats get information and understand their world with their extra-sensitive whiskers. The tip of each whisker identifies changes in the environment and sends messages to the brain.

These sensory hairs detect temperature, feel vibrations, and help cats "see" in the dark. Whiskers help cats judge the size of a narrow opening. Since cats can't see well up close or under their chin, they use their whiskers to feel for food.

Kitty Corner

If I fit, I sit!

My whiskers told me this box is the purr-fect size.

Why Are Cats...
SCAREDY-CATS?

Kitties are curious creatures—but they're also cautious and don't like change. And it's true; they scare easily.

Cats tend to feel threatened by loud noises and unfamiliar people. But if cats feel safe enough, they investigate something new.

If a cat can't escape a bad situation, it might lie down and fluff its tail. The cat's not showing its belly for a rub. Instead, it wants to look large. Cats fight as a last resort.

Mixed Breed

Tabby Cat

Kitty Corner

I felt threatened when you stared at me, but you looked away first. Now I know you're purr-fectly friendly.

11

WHY DO CATS PUFF THEIR TAILS?

Watch a cat to know how it feels.

If you notice a cat's tail twitching or wagging, the cat may feel uneasy or be on the prowl.

A scared cat puffs its tail to look larger. He even pulls his whiskers back toward his body to protect them from harm.

Watch the cat's ears, too. The ears might flatten in anger or turn sideways to listen closely. A stressed cat pulls back her ears. An anxious cat's ears might move back and forth or be stiff. A relaxed cat's ears stand up and face forward.

Watch my tail when I come close. If it's straight up like a flagpole, that's my signal that I think you're **paw-some.**

CAT'S TAIL LANGUAGE

Scared

Uneasy

Friendly

Cautious

Relaxed

Anxious

Black Kitten

13

Why Do Cats Hunt?

Cats need meat since their bodies cannot make protein. They get meat from cat food—or by hunting. Protein is their most important source of energy.

In the wild, cats hunt animals like rodents, insects, fish, and birds. Experienced hunters also feast on frogs, lizards, and squirrels.

Once the cat spots her prey, she waits—crouched and nearly motionless. Then...

POUNCE!

The cat's teeth stab and slice through the food—but the meal is swallowed and digested without chewing.

Kitty Corner

I love a bit of catnip or cat grass, but I don't need fruits and veggies in my diet. Grapes and garlic make me sick. Feeding me those would be un-fur-tunate!

How Do Cats Land On Their Paws?

Cats have exceptional balance and quick reflexes. Inside their ears are hairs that help them to sense which way is up. As a cat falls, it twists and turns its body to stay upright.

When a cat is in mid-air, it rotates its head and shoulders in one direction while its backside spins the opposite way. Before landing, cats extend their legs and arch their backs to cushion the fall. Even their tails help them balance.

Amazingly, cats nearly always land on their paws. Though they don't really have nine lives like the myth says, quick reflexes get them out of tough situations.

Brown Tabby

Kitty Corner

Are you "kitten" me?
Olympic gymnasts have nothing on these feline feet.

WHAT'S THAT SMELL?

Domestic cats come from desert-dwelling African wildcats. So, our pet cats use most of the water they drink to stay hydrated. That leaves their urine super concentrated—and super smelly from the protein they eat.

Cat urine includes important information for other cats. Pungent pee means the cat is an especially successful hunter (or gets high-quality cat food at home). So, a female cat chooses the male with the strongest odor as her mate.

Some people think cats are descended from lions. That's not true. They are descended from a species of African wildcat called *Felis lybica*.

Kitty Corner

You call it a marking, but I call it a meow-velous message. Other male cats smell my scent signals, which are called pheromones.

Now they know to stay away from my space.

19

Why Is My Cat Acting This Way?

British Shorthair

Cats show us plenty of puzzling behaviors. Some of what cats do might annoy us, but mostly they're just being a cat.

Cats often scratch furniture and even walls. They do this because their claws are always growing. Scratching also calms cats and leaves their communication scents called pheromones behind. To prevent unwanted scratching, you can trim the nails and give your cat a tall scratching post. It might stop the scratching. But it might not.

As natural hunters, cats sometimes play with their catch. They might be trying to figure out how to kill it, or they might be weakening the prey so it won't fight back. The hunting instinct is so strong, often outdoor cats hunt prey without eating the catch.

If your cat suddenly begins doing something new, like hissing, scratching, or not using the litter box, it's time to visit a veterinarian. About half of the unwanted behaviors vets see are related to medical issues.

I like you, but sometimes I need to be alone. It's my cat-titude.

How do Cats Communicate?

MEOW. MEOW. MEOW.

HISS. HISS. HISS.

Bengal Cat

Sphynx Cat

22

British Shorthair

PURR. PURR. PURR.

Purrrrrrrr!

We don't have to stop purring to take a breath. Just pet me—fur-ever—or until I walk away.

Kittens and cats purr when they're happy. But they also purr when they are hungry, sick, or in pain. The vibration of muscles in their voice box makes the purring sound.

Cats tend to meow for people—not other cats. Cats change their meows for different situations. Some meows say, "Pay attention to me!" or even, "Open this door!" An angry meow sounds different from a meow for affection.

They communicate with other sounds, too. Your cat's trill might sound a bit like a question. It can be a greeting to a friend or an invitation to follow. A hiss warns of their anger. It might be paired with a growl.

23

How Do Cats Show They Care?

Some people think cats don't care about people because they're not as expressive as some animals. But they do show affection. Every time a cat rubs against your legs, it says "hello." The cat's scent also rubs off on you—this scent marking tells other cats that you're a good friend.

Our feline friends show affection in other ways, too. Slow blinks show cats are calm. Like a smile, it's an act of friendliness or contentment. Cats often lick others with their tongues. They groom other cats, animals, and even people. It's one way they take care of us.

Cats jump on couches, beds, and counters to be near to us.
Some cats hear a familiar voice and come running with...

THE SWISHING TAIL.

THE TWITCHING EARS.

THE RUMBLING PURR.

AND THAT'S THE TRUTH ABOUT CATS.

Kitty Corner

I thought you might be hungry.

Here's a mouse I caught just for you, my purr-y friend!

25

COMMON CAT COAT PATTERNS

Cats' coats come in a variety of color patterns and fur markings. Here are some general groupings.

Calico and Tortoise Shell

multiple-colored patches include orange, black, and white

Solid

all one color

Tabby

stripes, spots, lines, or swirls throughout fur

Tuxedo

white markings on chest, belly, and paws

Points

darker coloring on the paws, ears, tail, and nose

Kinds of Kitties

Most pet cats don't come from a recognized breed. We just call them domestic cats.

Coat color and patterns, body and head shape, and eye shape and color are some of the characteristics different cat registries use to determine recognized cat breeds.

The International Cat Association recognizes more than 70 different breeds of cats.

(Other registries count more than 100 breeds.)

Lykoi, Werewolf Cat

American Ringtails are playful and have a tail that curls.

Siamese are born all-white and develop color points on their paws, ears, tail, and nose.

Bombays are all black like a miniature panther and very playful.

American Shorthairs make good companions for children and get along with other animals.

(They are a specific breed within the most common American pet cat grouping called domestic shorthairs.)

Longhair Cats

Persians have long, thick coats and a flat face and like to relax.

Maine Coons are known for their massive size though they play like kittens, even as adults.

Ragdolls go limp when picked up and are known to follow their owners like a dog.

Hairless Cat

Sphynx have fuzzy skin and are known for being social and active.

Fascinating Feline Facts

Extra Toes

Most cats have five toes on their front paws and four on their back paws. But some cats are born with extra toes. It's a genetic trait called polydactylism.

The Ernest Hemmingway Home & Museum on the small island of Key West, Florida is home to 60 polydactyl cats.

Purrs and Roars

Cats can either purr or roar. They cannot do both. It all depends on their voice boxes. Tigers, lions, leopards, and jaguars all roar, but not because of their large size. Roaring cats have a stretchy ligament in their voice box. Wild cats like cheetahs, mountain lions, and lynx purr like our domestic house cats. The bone in their voice box vibrates and creates a purring sound.

Unwelcomed Pests

Overpopulation concerns many cat lovers, but in some countries and cultures cats are disliked, especially feral (wild) populations. For example, cats are more of a pest than a pleasure—and rarely a pet—in Israel. Some people in Vietnam consider feral cats bad luck. Myths, superstitions, and folklore often include cats.

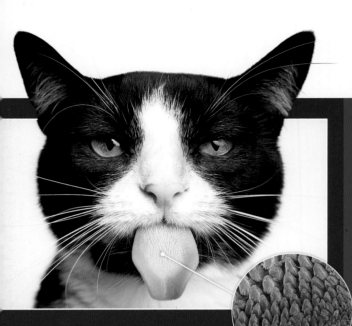

POPULATION CONTROL

One pair of adult cats can have 4–6 kittens in a litter. Even if less than two kittens in a litter become adults, the original two cats and all their offspring and offspring's offspring would create 100 cats in just seven years.*

However, many cats produce two litters a year. Two cats and their descendants would number 5,000 in just seven years if they had two litters each year!

BLUE-EYED BABIES

All cats are born with blue eyes. The irises slowly change to the adult colors of gold, green, brown, or sometimes dark blue as the cat matures.

THE TOOL TONGUE

Cat tongues do more than drink and taste. Cat tongues feel like sandpaper because of curved barbs called papillae covering the cat's tongue.

Papillae are extremely useful for eating, especially when cleaning bones in the wild. Cats bathe frequently. The papillae on their tongues remove dirt and dander in the fur and clean the skin.

Most cats do not need help grooming or bathing regularly. However, longhaired cats such as Persians need to be brushed daily to prevent matted fur.

Spay and neuter your cats to prevent overpopulation.

* Each diagram represents a male and female pair of cats who are not spayed or neutered and all their offspring. Numbers are based on cats having 1.75 living offspring with each litter.

1 LITTER PER YEAR
1 Year: 4 cats
2 Years: 6 cats
3 Years: 11 cats
4 Years: 19 cats
5 Years: 33 cats
6 Years: 58 cats
7 Years: 101 cats

2 LITTERS PER YEAR
1 Year: 6 cats
2 Years: 19 cats
3 Years: 56 cats
4 Years: 176 cats
5 Years: 539 cats
6 Years: 1,650 cats
7 Years: 5,043 cats

29

LEFTY OR RIGHTY?

Most people prefer to use one hand over the other. We say the preferred hand is the dominant hand. Do you think your cat has a dominant paw? Make a guess and research with your cat over several days to find out.

Cats do not always cooperate with scientific research. If your cat loses interest, continue collecting information on another day. It might be helpful to research when your cat is most active, likely at dawn and dusk.

You'll Need:

- treats
- pen or pencil
- paper

Note: As you look at your cat from the front, its left and right sides are opposite of yours. If you watch your cat from behind, its left and right sides match your own.

❶ Get Ready:

Create a chart with three columns. Label the columns "Test," "Left," and "Right." Number the rows 1–20. Title the chart "Treat Test."

Treat Test		
Test	Left	Right
1.		
2.		
3.		
4.		
5.		

❷ Treat Test

Place a treat under a piece of furniture where your cat can reach it with some effort. (The cat should not be able to crawl under the furniture.) In the "Test" column, write a name for this test, such as "coffee table." Show your cat the treat. Note on the chart if your cat used its left or right paw by marking the appropriate column. Repeat the test multiple times. Circle the marks to show your cat successfully grabbed the treat. Move the treat so it isn't always easy or hard for your cat to reach it.

What Did You Learn?

Examine the results. Based on the information you gathered, what did you learn? Which is your cat's dominant paw? Or could the cat be ambidextrous, like some humans who use both hands equally? Do you think any testing needs to be repeated or changed? Change locations to another piece of furniture or use a door for variety. Record until you have at least 15–20 swipes total (or until your cat loses interest). Expect your cat to earn many treats.

Glossary

digest: to eat food and make it usable for energy

domestic: living near or with humans

feline: any animal in the cat family

feral: untamed or living in the wild

genetic: related to family and ancestors

instinct: a natural behavior that is not learned

papillae: small bumps or spines on the tongue which help grip food and clean

pheromone: a chemical scent that tells information to the same species of animal

protein: plant or animal parts that make a good food source

pungent: having a strong smell or taste

reflex: an automatic behavior that does not need to be learned

scruff: the loose skin on the back of the neck

sensory: able to send and receive information

Some Helpful Websites

www.animalhumanesociety.org

www.aspca.org

www.cfa.org

https://indoorpet.osu.edu

www.tica.org

Meet Annette Whipple

Annette Whipple celebrates curiosity and inspires a sense of wonder while exciting readers about science and history. She's the author of 12 fact-filled children's books, including *Whooo Knew? The Truth About Owls* and other books in The Truth About series. When Annette's not reading or writing, you might find her baking. She lives in Pennsylvania with her family, including two cats named Kiwi and Soka.